Richard Wilson

Jamming Gears

Serpentine Gallery 1996

Sponsor's Foreword

We are extremely proud to launch our support of the Arts by sponsoring Richard Wilson's innovative exhibition at the Serpentine Gallery.

Richard Wilson's exciting installation *Jamming Gears* provokes us to think afresh about the spaces we inhabit and the feelings they engender, in the light of the Serpentine Gallery's imminent renovation.

This marks a new beginning in a long term commitment to the Arts and we are delighted to associate our name with the Serpentine Gallery and its aspirations.

Vittorio Radice

Managing Director

Selfridges

Foreword

This is the last exhibition at the Serpentine Gallery before the building closes for extensive refurbishment, and thus constitutes the finale of our current programme. It is very fitting that it should be a new installation by the renowned British artist Richard Wilson, given his unique approach to existing architecture which has resulted in some of the strongest visual statements in contemporary art practice. There is undeniable drama in Wilson's rearrangement of component parts of a building, the intersection and juxtaposition of these with objects and materials derived from other contexts, and a sheer delight in incongruity. This foils the artist's subtle investigations into the nature not only of what it is we actually construct but also what these constructions signify particularly in terms of an all-too-human need for certainty in a world of ceaseless change. Without doubt this exhibition alludes to the imminent transformation of the Serpentine Gallery, but clearly there is so much more beyond this particular situation which it has to offer.

This installation is a generous work and also the result of much generosity. Above all we thank Richard Wilson for his extraordinary vision, commitment and enthusiasm, and with him take this opportunity to acknowledge other contributions made by a considerable number of individuals and organisations; without them the overall result of this project would have been much harder, if not impossible, to achieve. The sponsorship of Selfridges, in association with The Guardian, is of great benefit and most imaginative. The support of The Henry Moore Foundation, The Andy Warhol Foundation, Lansing Linde Ltd, Kilnbridge Construction Ltd and Channel Four Television is very gratefully received.

Alan Broughton (Howard Associates), from the start of the preparations for this exhibition, has been unstinting in his consultation and practical advice. Likewise the expertise of Colin Smith and Ray Crouch (Davis Langdon Management), Tom Smith and Adrian Tooth (WSP Consulting Engineers), John Carpenter (John Miller +

Partners) has been invaluable. Roberto Ruggieri, Carl von Weiler and Tim Wilson, with the Serpentine Gallery's technical staff, have worked beyond the call of duty, with great skill and dedication.

Finally, it remains for us to thank Silvia Ziranek for her thoughtfulness and Robin Klassnik who, with Simon Morrissey at Matt's Gallery, has helped enormously with every aspect of this exhibition.

Jonathan Watkins
Curator

Julia Peyton-Jones
Director

Jamming Gears

You are on a boat going down a river. You are a stranger to these parts; a tourist on a sight-seeing trip. The guide tells you the history that shores up the landmarks that you are passing by. The guide is bored, perhaps a little bit tired, maybe he forgets his lines. Every now and again he stops telling the truth. As a stranger to this part of London you are not aware of what he is doing. He is the guide taking you down the river. You accept what he says as truth and whatever he says makes you see the riverscape in a new way. It has been explained. You now believe that you know what the buildings were built for, what events happened around them, who lived there. You point your camera at these buildings and take photographs that you will later show to your friends and family when you get home. You tell them those same stories again.

Having experienced such a trip, Richard Wilson arrived, in May 1995, at the Negeb Desert in southern Israel. Using two postcards of the desert, bought at a nearby tourist office, he constructed a miniature screen. One postcard was cut-up to provide the supports for the other which became both the actual screen and half of its image. Onto this postcard/screen, showing the surrounding desert landscape, he projected a slide from his trip up the River Thames that showed the view towards Tower Bridge. The bridge and the riverbank float, mirage-like on the image of the desert (the desert had at one time been covered by water). In the background could be heard a tape-loop recording of the guide's commentary.

Between the projection of a play of belief, artifice and truth, *Pleasure Trip* 1995 encapsulates, on such a very small scale, many of the concerns and themes that Wilson explores in his work. Although much of this work is considered to be paradigmatic of a strategy of spatial intervention or installation, what *Pleasure Trip* immediately highlights is the degree to which one of his foremost concerns can be located by an attention to the ways that art, portrayed as conveying an idea of truth, is actually formed out of artifice. The object, positioned and held in space, might deliver a welcome degree of tangibility (a postcard and the cast of projected light). However, this reaction is undercut by the image thrown out by the object, and by the ways in which that image is perceived and looked at when such an objectively defined space is entered. Such a dichotomy lies as one key to Wilson's work: between interior and exterior spaces, the home and the work-place, the object and the image, the real and the artificially contrived, between that which is projected and seen or that which is experienced and felt. He has created a body of work that, while it is informed by a process of transformation (of materials as much as within the language of perception), should only be judged in terms of a finished presentation in which its reception becomes a temporal event. Over ten years ago Wilson had admitted the extent to which the River Thames was a useful example to him in helping to understand the ways in which perception of one's imme-diate surroundings is determined by the passage of time: "The con-stant in and out of the tide, along with those rapid changes of the waterfront. The only thing which, once upon a time, moved upon the river was the water. The water seems to have stopped and every-thing else around it is really busy. So it's that impermanence of one's direct environment."[1]

A useful parallel can be found in Maurice Blanchot's analysis of imagination, in which he suggests that, even though an awareness of the object precedes the image, it is at the point at which the image is located that the play of artifice interlocks with sight so as to separate the two. "The thing was there; we grasped it in the vital movement of a comprehensive action – and lo, having become image, instantly it has become that which no one can grasp, the unreal, the impossible. It is not the same thing at a distance but the thing as distance, pre-sent in its absence, graspable because ungraspable, appearing as disappeared."[2] It is at such a point, "graspable because ungras-pable", that *Pleasure Trip* is made both real and fictive; a point where

1 Richard Wilson interviewed by Lynne Cooke in *Heatwave*, Ikon Gallery, Birmingham 1985, p. 10.
2 Maurice Blanchot, *The Space of Literature*, University of Nebraska Press, Lincoln 1989, pp. 255–256.

the awareness of the object slips into a temporal event of perception of the image. A postcard of the desert becomes a screen for the projected play of a conceit in which Tower Bridge is found in the shrunken image of an Israeli desert that echoes the existence of London Bridge in Arizona.[3] Furthermore, the confined space of the air-raid shelter, in which the work was housed, provided a counterpoint to the wilderness outside, that was itself reduced in scale and pictured in the postcard and subjected to the specific pictorial metaphor of a transportation, and dislocation, of cultural language. The play, within perception, between object, image, metaphor and artifice, colours much of Wilson's work. *20:50* 1987, for instance, presents an expanse of sump oil divided by a narrow passage. This black, dirty, substance becomes a voided field that mirrors the ceiling suggesting that the beholder might be suspended, weightlessly, in space rather than hemmed-in by oil. The further one goes down the passage, the more illusory, and believably real, is the experience.

This projection of perceptual confusion had been at the heart of a work, made two years later. Wilson removed one of the gallery windows from Matt's Gallery, moved it into the gallery space and positioned it at an angle from the wall, and then created false walls rather like a camera bellows that held the window within the gallery space and projected outside the gallery into what had originally been the view from the window.[4] *She Came in Through the Bathroom Window* 1989 is concerned as much with a displacement from what had been looked through to something that one looks at, as with what happens when an interior space is projected into an exterior space by virtue of that temporary shifting of a room's boundary line. This displacement of types of visuality is again played-out against

3 The apocryphal story being that, when sold, the buyer erroneously believed that it was Tower Bridge that was going to be dismantled and shipped to Arizona.
4 Three years later Wilson expanded on this idea when, with *Return to Sender* 1992 exhibited at the Galerie de l'Ancienne Poste in Calais, he projected the mullions and transoms of one of the windows into the gallery space and stood them on the same radiator that had originally been under the window but had also been projected into the room and turned on its side. Between the gaps that then existed in the window frame, and the mullions and transoms, Wilson built an acrylic sheathing that still let the cold air in above the working radiator.

a bridging of a set of dichotomies between object and the sensed image, between that which is "seized upon *with* the eyes" and that which is "seized on *by* the senses"[5] which itself is also presented as a visualised movement from the inside of the gallery to what lies outside. The beholder's apprehension of *She Came in Through the Bathroom Window* as an object might therefore be purely visual but a proper perception of the work involves a bodily movement, guided by sight, into a space that had been changed and that itself changed the way we look. Looking at anything in this way "is to inhabit it, and from this habitation to grasp all things in terms of the aspect which they present to it."[6] Moving in, we inhabit the gallery as the window has also come to. We look at it, through it to where it used to be, and beyond to the view that it had previously looked out on. We see the object (the window that had been moved and the resulting room that this change has made). We sense something else.

The extent to which this sense of habitation can be found to be suggested through Wilson's work is aided, not only by the often domestic, or homely, metaphors that he sometimes deploys (a bathroom window, a greenhouse, a kit-built chalet, a hotel room, a chair or a caravan), but also by the way in which recourse is often made to an idea of a plinth. This is not to say that he sites his work on an actual plinth (although in some works, such as *Deep End* 1995, compositional elements do form plinth-like connections to the space of the viewer) but rather that the room itself can offer the qualities of a plinth to whatever Wilson might do to it. In this he joins with the post-war history of sculpture which dispensed with the plinth as a function of elevating and isolating sculpture from the world surrounding it, in favour of an "expanded field". Located in real space, without a plinth that had provided sculpture with a denotative function, the work had to provide its own designating function. Where such strategies might coincide with an increasing autonomy of artistic practice, Wilson has used the room – space and our means of

5 Maurice Merleau-Ponty, *Phenomenology of Perception,* Routledge & Kegan Paul, London 1989, pp. 6 and 7.
6 *Ibid.* p. 68.

perceiving space – as a way of denoting and defining the work which, itself, includes space and the event of perception as a part of its fabric.

Elbow Room 1993, *Room 6 Channel View Hotel* 1996, *High Rise* 1989 and *Deep End* 1995 suggest how he has realised this. All four works exist as a disruption of the gallery by domestic spaces that have a generic status – the chalet, the hotel room, the greenhouse and the swimming-pool – so that one's perception of the work is immediately formed by this movement from the personal and the particular to the impersonal, the public and the generalised. *Elbow Room* had been made for Oslo's Museet for Samtidskunst – a building that had originally been a bank. Unable to tamper with the fabric of the room in any way Wilson created a surrogate portion of floor and wall that banked-up, as if perspectivally foreshortened. Behind the wall, as if propping it up, he inserted a section from an Ikea-type kit-build chalet and so provided a view that had been hidden by the wall and, at the same time, a stereotyped view of a Scandinavian life-style – all stripped-pine saunas and chalets. The plinth to this work is difficult to locate as each possible location does not denote the work, so much as mark a perceptual passage from untouched gallery, to artificial section of gallery, to section of a domestic space, which is always both exterior and interior. Beyond suggesting that the plinth might be the observer moving through this set of experiences, perhaps the plinth might exist as well as an awareness of metaphor. And this sensing of metaphor provides Wilson's body of work with another set of meanings by which it can be negotiated by the beholder.

In a similar way to the situation that led to *Elbow Room*, the fabric of the space that housed *Room 6 Channel View Hotel* – the Towner Art Gallery in Eastbourne – could also not be tampered with by Wilson. Into this room he inserted a linear diagram of the hotel room in which he had stayed while making the work. This diagram, constructed out of lengths of Dexion Speedframe, was mounted on casters and raised up enough from the floor so as to be slightly disorienting. The projection of its ceiling, with its boxed representation of light fittings, overlapped with the gallery's own suspended lighting track. Where the casters suggest a feeling of mobility, the interlocking between the two ceilings conveys a degree of entrapment that is emphasised by the fact that we cannot enter the diagram, only walk around it. What the diagrammatic nature of the room provides the beholder with is the experience of being inside a room while looking at the inside of a diagram of another room, but from the outside. Even though one might wonder which is the more institutional space, the differences of type between the gallery room and the diagram of the hotel room are further defined by the photographs of personal effects that have been encased in perspex and, as it were, left to lie around the diagram. Where the bedroom is usually a domestic and intimate space, the hotel bedroom will always be impersonal, however much one might try to change it in trying to make each hotel room a surrogate for our own home.

The conflict that arises in *Elbow Room* and *Room 6 Channel View Hotel*, between exterior and interior, private and public, as well as between the different sorts of lifestyles these spaces project to us is emphasised again in *Deep End*, made for the Museum of Contemporary Art in Los Angeles. A ready-to-wear swimming pool is stood up, at an angle, with a pipe that rises vertically, from the pool's floor, to puncture the roof of the gallery and emerge into the polluted air of the city outside. Wilson has described the metaphorical charge he intends the work to provide as being one formed from the similar dualities and mechanics of perception that had been expressed in *Elbow Room*: "The idea of the pool came about while flying into LA International Airport, looking down, seeing all these sixties' modernist shapes of sky blue, and recognising that there were these peculiar lifestyles being lived out in the hills of Los Angeles ... With the pool, I was using an architectural element that engaged the body in a social, as well as a physical, way ... When you look through the pipe in *Deep End*, you see the blue sky of Los Angeles – the reality of the world as opposed to the artifice of the Bahamas blue, the paradise blue, of the swimming pool. The artificiality of the pool is supposed to represent an ideal lifestyle – paradise. Yet in *Deep End*, reality appears, as it were, up a drain pipe."[7] The plinth, such as it is, is formed as a connection between exterior and interior physical states as well as between the different perceptual responses to the object and image; between the Californian dream and its often grotesque reality. In this respect the pipe cannot be identified as the plinth, except through such metaphorical connectivity.

High Rise, like *Elbow Room*, places a building inside a building. However, where in Oslo the new wall, floor and chalet had been positioned in a room whose structural fabric had not been materially altered, *High Rise*'s greenhouse, glazed only at one end, punctures a beautifully made false wall that had been constructed for the São Paulo Bienal. An area of the surface of the wall, surrounding the point at which the wall had been ruptured by the greenhouse's insertion, was removed, revealing its structure to be temporary rather than load-bearing. Such an act reveals the gallery to be a place of artifice. An insecticutor draws the beholder towards the greenhouse and then around the other side, into a service corridor that would, more normally, be closed off from view. In other locations, where the work has been presented, it has punctured through into another gallery or into an office. In 1990, at Moscow's Central House of the Artist, *High Rise* had been inserted into a wall between the gallery space and a storage room that, itself, looked out onto a cityscape of Stalinist architecture; another order of artifice that was both socially and physically defining. The unsettling and extraordinary image of *High Rise* – a greenhouse, mounted at an angle, high up, cleanly penetrating a wall that is revealed to be little more than an insubstantial screen – provides a narrative of a perception of materials and space as much as of sight and hidden structures. Furthermore, the immaculate physicality of the work paradoxically leads the beholder to confront the fragile, open form, of the greenhouse, and what it is doing in, and to, the gallery space, in less literal and more metaphorical and perceptual ways.

7 Paul Schimmel, 'Interview with Richard Wilson', *Richard Wilson. Deep End*, The British Council, London/ Museum of Contemporary Art, Los Angeles 1995, pp.13 and 15.

In this respect, and like *Deep End*, *High Rise* leads one to question the conjunction of artifice and the real.[8] The greenhouse is a building that is both "urban and rural, temporary and permanent, part of house and garden, they exist midway between nature and culture, the wild and the cultivated."[9] Wilson has often used objects that contain such an ambiguous range of reference as a way of pitching the artifice of art against the world outside in a context that is perceptually loaded towards real experience. Real objects are transformed into something else but the resulting image is still accepted as a form of truth, "graspable because ungraspable"; a form of truth that is only recognisable and perceivable as a result of its negation through artifice and the act of transformation.

To these ends, Wilson's work joins together a material transformation with a perceptual transformation that takes place through sight and in time. In 1985 Wilson stated that "maybe one of the first pieces which really excited me was the *Standard Stoppages* by Duchamp. The fact that one could drop pieces of string and make work which was about time and change; one could find new ways of logging actions."[10] Although Duchamp understood these measuring rods, that duplicated the forms achieved after having dropped a metre long thread from a height of one metre, as an attempt to "imprison and preserve forms obtained through chance",[11] it is significant that Wilson's interest in the work was directed towards the performative event and the relationship it might hold towards the

8 *Leading Lights* 1989, installed at the Kunsthallen Brandts Klædefabrik in Odense in Southern Denmark, offers another commentary on the natural/artificial and interior/exterior dichotomies in Wilson's work in a way that focuses much more on the perceptual mechanics of sight. For this work he took the 84 light-bulbs that illuminated one floor of a warehouse gallery space and placed them all at one window – a point of transition between the interior gallery space and the port of Odense that exists outside the building. This positioning not only provided a source of heat against the cold winter exterior but also emphasised the provision of an artificial light at a time of year and geographical location where there was only four hours of natural daylight each day.

9 Sarah Kent, *Shark Infested Waters,* Zwemmer/Philip Wilson Publishers Ltd, London 1994, p.110.

10 Richard Wilson interviewed by Lynne Cooke, 1985, *op. cit.*, p.10.

11 Marcel Duchamp, 'Apropos of Myself', lecture delivered at the City Art Museum of St Louis, Missouri on November 24, 1964, printed in Anne d'Harnoncourt & Kynaston McShine (eds.), *Marcel Duchamp*, Museum of Modern Art, New York 1973, p.273.

perceptual act. Some of Wilson's earliest exhibited works, such as *Twelve Pieces* 1977 or *Wind Instruments* 1980, both of which were shown by Coracle Press, were sculptures whose component parts existed in a box. The sculptures could then be assembled and displayed, or packed-up and stored-away as required. This temporal basis to perception as analogous with the act of creative transformation is a theme that can be continually identified in his subsequent work.

One aspect of this relationship is the position that is given to process within the act of transformation. Much installation art that declares its autonomy does this by referencing the process of fabrication within its structure as a means of displaying its separateness. Although many of Wilson's early sculptures and work of the 1980s incorporated materials that had obviously undergone direct physical change – cast aluminium in *Big Dipper* 1982, *Viaduct* 1983 and *Sheer Fluke* 1984–85, water in *Hopperhead* 1985, gas flame in *Hot Live Still* 1987 or falling auto-parts and sound recording in *One Piece at a Time* 1987 – the beholder was, more often than not, left with an object from which the theatre of process could be recognised even though immediate evidence for this had been largely cleared away. *One Piece at a Time* was one of the few works that included a direct performative element within the work's structure and parallels Wilson's involvement, during this period, with Anne Bean and Paul Burwell as the Bow Gamelan performance group.[12] Since the disbanding of this group in 1990 Wilson's work has pushed this evidently process-based and performative element aside, even though the transformations that have been wrought might seem just as great. All of his work is formed out of processes that are, by and large, effaced within the beholder's perception of the work. The often heavy manual labour disappears from sight through Wilson's lightness of touch, that creates objects and situations that seem to have been always already there; it is in this way that the object can slip towards the image.

12 The Bow Gamelan Group used discarded industrially formed objects, as well as fire, to create experimental musical sound.

Much more than the transformation of the site (or the transformation of objects held within that site) is the transformation that is read by the beholder through the act of seeing and experiencing this shift from object to image (from dark, impenetrable, oil to weightless suspension in *20:50*, for example). One of the few recent works in which a material process of working is directly referenced is found in *Formative Processes* 1996, the structure constructed for the display of drawings and maquettes at Gimpel Fils. These drawings – ranging from schematic diagrams, pictorial projections and rougher notations – trace the thought processes that Wilson follows in conceiving these works. By presenting the drawings on a structure that is reminiscent of the hoardings that surround building sites, one aspect of *Formative Processes* recalls the major material transformation that Wilson's work has to undergo while it is being fabricated. However, the individual drawings are contained, recessed into the hoarding, within windows that are not unlike those viewing holes that surround building sites allowing one to occupy a view and see what changes are occurring behind those screens. In this respect *Formative Processes* again reveals the extent to which Wilson's work is born out of this dual transformation – of material object and sensed image – that is locked together and pulls apart through the act of perception.

These viewing holes return one to the cinematic nature of Wilson's achievement. It is not that his work is always large, such a judgement is not of great significant value here as *Pleasure Trip* has shown. Gaston Bachelard's belief was that, when considering the conjunction between "inside" and "outside" (a conjunction that is a constant thread in Wilson's work): "Everything, even size, is a human value ... the miniature can accumulate size. It is vast in its way".[13] It is the wavering distances between these metaphorical and actual dichotomies within Wilson's work – framed by the perceptual shift between object and image – that creates size. From another corresponding angle is the example of the effect of artifice and spectacle within cinematic composition where belief is caught within the frame

13 Gaston Bachelard, *The Poetics of Space,* Beacon Press, Boston 1994, p. 215.

of the camera's viewfinder. Take the eye away, move around the film set, and belief falls away as everything is seen for what it is. However, such an event rarely occurs in Wilson's work. Even if we are made aware of the artifice, this belief continues to exert its pull because of the intangible connection that Wilson projects between an object and the way in which it is perceived as image through the manipulation of qualities of site.

Not too clear on the viewfinder 1992–93 provides one illustration of this condition. As preparation for his contribution to the 1993 Sydney Biennale Wilson was sent a video-tape tour of the room that he had been allocated. When he viewed the tape it was found to consist of an indistinct and darkened picture, accompanied by a commentary that complained of a lack of light while, at the same time, attempting to give an indication of the room's characteristics. A transcript was made of the tape and this was etched into the surface of a pair of huge fire doors that separated Wilson's space from the rest of the gallery building. The doors were moved into the room and suspended from the ceiling and a bright light directed at the doors, thus making the letters shimmer and the whole text be unreadable from a single viewing position. One had to move around the space to be able to read a description of a failure to communicate the nature of the space. Object and image were in this way brought together and thrown apart.

The pairing of fork-lift trucks with building-site huts might, on first impression, suggest that Wilson's newest work, *Jamming Gears*, has turned the Serpentine Gallery into a building site. Nevertheless, very little building work or, for that matter, destruction has actually taken place beyond the drilling of seven bore holes and the digging of a rectangular pit that provides the foundation for one of the site-huts. More pertinent are the ways *Jamming Gears* attempts to take a measure to the perceptual act, between exposing the structural mechanics of display and the institutional demands, in a gallery, of a circulation of sight. The core-drilling summons up a structural history, rather like a section through an archaeological dig, while at the same time pointing to the essential fragility and artificiality of that structure's intentions. Entering through the portico entrance, the north gallery contains just one drilled hole in the floor. From this viewpoint it is impossible to see exactly how deep it is. Closer, it can be seen just how near the soil layer is to the surface; providing an image that puts the structural stability of the Serpentine Gallery immediately into question.

The three, acidly lime-green, site-huts, two of which are supported by the red fork-lift trucks, are arranged in each of the other galleries. They become sight-huts in a way that parallels Wilson's use of a similar hut in *Doner* 1996 at the Barcelona Museu d'Art Contemporani. Through their transformed state, and assisted by the fork-lift trucks, the beholder is directed in seeing the site anew. Where in Barcelona, although there was no fork-lift truck, the hut was supposedly held up by a pair of elongated forks that pierced both the internal and external walls of the gallery to reach at the hut. Here, at the Serpentine, it is not the forks but the huts themselves that break into and out of the space.

In the Serpentine's west gallery the hut is suspended upside down in a pit that has been cut into the floor of the gallery. The hut's own floor has been cut away to reveal its ceiling as a new floor. In the east gallery the hut has been pushed by the truck into the gallery's French-windows – the window-frames taking the place of the hut's own walls. In the south gallery the hut has been raised up at one end. This hut has been studded with five holes from which cores, drilled from the Serpentine's fabric, protrude. What the cores have revealed can be glimpsed through the door of the hut that, having been raised up, has flapped open.

Jamming Gears, like much of Wilson's work provides a site for hidden spaces to be seen. *watertable* 1994, had suggested that the solid foundations of Matt's Gallery lay on nothing more substantial than an expanse of water lapping around the legs of the billiard table, that had itself been sunk in a pit in the gallery – the baize surface of the cushions level with the gallery's floor surface. A seventh hole – a water pipe – in the billiard table provided a well to this other, liquid, table. *Pleasure Trip* had projected the seemingly ridiculous image of water in the Negeb desert. *Jamming Gears*, does not just take as its hidden material the spaces between walls or under the floors, but also seeks to find a hidden space of sight. Not satisfied with just revealing that there are physical spaces that are hidden, Wilson here, as elsewhere, attempts to provide the space for a perceptual experience that might itself be out of reach. The object might exist, believable, immediate and tangible but, as soon as that is grasped, the image leads the beholder elsewhere. This dichotomy, so important to Wilson, between internal and external spaces, acts persuasively not just in terms of the actual physical object but the ways in which they are perceived, "*with* the eyes" and "*by* the senses". We see a space that has had its boundaries physically transgressed and yet the image our senses hold onto is one framed by a belief in material truth.

In the Preface to his *Phenomenology of Perception*, Merleau-Ponty makes the suggestion that just as the "... phenomenological world is not the bringing to explicit expression of a pre-existing being, but the laying down of being. Philosophy is not the reflection of a pre-existing truth, but, like art, the act of bringing truth into being."[14] Wilson's work shows that such truth, formed out of artifice, cannot be materially defined but only experienced as a temporal encounter with the object, as the movement of seeing a changing site. Such truth – and in this respect art is both "exile from truth"[15] and duplicitous – does not provide certainty or an exact measure, but impels the beholder to ask questions of the site and of the seeing.

Andrew Wilson
Summer 1996

14 Maurice Merleau-Ponty, 1989, *op. cit.,* p. xx.
15 Maurice Blanchot, 1989, *op. cit.,* p. 240.

Select Bibliography

1985
Mel Gooding, 'Richard Wilson at Matt's Gallery',
Artscribe, no. 51, March – April;
Michael Newman, 'From Inside the Whale', *Artforum*,
Summer

1986
Lynne Cooke, interview, *Heatwave*, exhibition
catalogue, Ikon Gallery, Birmingham;
Chrissie Iles, 'Suspended Animation', *Performance*,
no. 43, September – October

1987
Michael Archer, 'Richard Wilson's 20:50', *Art
Monthly*, no.104, March;
Gray Watson, 'Richard Wilson: Matt's Gallery,
Artscribe International, May;
Richard Cork, 'Beyond the Tyranny of the
Predictable', *TSWA 3D*, exhibition catalogue,
TSWA Ltd. London;
Mel Gooding, 'Seeing the Siter', *Art Monthly*, no. 108,
July–August;
Richard Cork, 'Site Reading: British Art in Public
Spaces', *Art in America*, September

1989
Michael Newman, 'From the Fire to the Light:
On Richard Wilson's Installations', *Richard Wilson*,
exhibition catalogue, Arnolfini Gallery, Bristol,
MOMA, Oxford and Matt's Gallery, London
Jeff Instone, 'Wilson, 'Wysiwyg' and Matt's Edge',
Art Monthly, no. 126, May;
Rick Poyner, 'Space Planner', *Blueprint*, no. 57, May;
Michael Archer, 'Richard Wilson', *Artforum*, no. 10,
Summer;
Oliver Bennett, 'Richard Wilson', *New Art Examiner*,
June;
Greg Hilty, 'Richard Wilson: Matt's Gallery', *Arena*,
no. 3, June;
Anne Grant, 'Richard Wilson: New Installations in
London, Oxford and Bristol', *Alba*, Summer;
Phoebe Tait, 'Richard Wilson', *Flash Art*, no. 147,
Summer;
James Roberts, 'Richard Wilson: Matt's Gallery,
London', *Artefactum*, vol. 6. no. 29, June–August;
'Richard Wilson', *Forty under Forty*, special edition of
Art and Design, vol. 5 no. 3–4;
Andrew Graham-Dixon, 'Neo, No: Still Faithful to the
Old Guard', *Art News*, vol. 88, no. 7, September;
Nicholas Wegner, 'Richard Wilson: Site Specific
Sculptor', interview, *CV*, vol. 2, no. 3, September

1991
Mauro Panzera, 'Richard Wilson: Milano, Galleria
Valeria Belvedere, 1991', *Titolo*, No. 6, Autumn

1992
Elio Grazioli, 'The Artful Lodger', *Annual Casa*;
Elisabeth Lebovici, 'Une Bonne Tranche de Richard
Wilson', *Libération*, 27 February;
Keiko Koyama, 'European Design Spirits', *Euro
Pronto*, vol. 2, no. 3.;
Maïten Bouisset, 'Richard Wilson', *Beaux Arts*,
no. 100, April;
Regine Pachner, 'Wilson', *Kanal Europe*, no. 2,
April– May

1993
James Roberts, 'Richard Wilson: Assembly
Required', *Threshold*, no. 9, January;
James Roberts, 'Richard Wilson', *Richard Wilson*,
exhibition catalogue, DAAD, Berlin;
Yuko Haswgawa, 'Richard Wilson', *Mito Annual '93:
Another World*, exhibition catalogue, Art Tower
Mito – Contemporary Art Gallery, Mito, Japan

1994
Michael Archer, 'Richard Wilson', *Artforum*, May;
Steve Rushton, 'Interview: By Digging you Discover',
Everything. London Artists Magazine, no. 14,
June–July;
Edward Winters, 'Richard Wilson's *watertable*',
Modern Painters, Summer;
Paul Schimmel, 'Interview with Richard Wilson',
Deep End, exhibition catalogue, MOCA, Los Angeles;
Shark Infested Waters, compiled by Jenny Blyth, text
Sarah Kent, Zwemmer / Philip Wilson Publishers Ltd.,
London;
Nicholas de Oliveira, Nicola Oxley, Michael Petry
(eds.), *Installation Art*, text Michael Archer, Thames
and Hudson, London

1995
Jeremy Till, interview, *Artifice*, Issue 2;
Yves Abrioux, 'Richard Wilson: Matt's Gallery',
Untitled, no. 5, Summer

1996
Ian Hunt, 'Richard Wilson: Towner Art Gallery
Eastbourne', *Art Monthly*, no. 197, June

Catalogue

She Came in Through the Bathroom Window 1989

High Rise 1989

26 **Lodger** 1991

28   **Elbow Room** 1993

watertable 1994

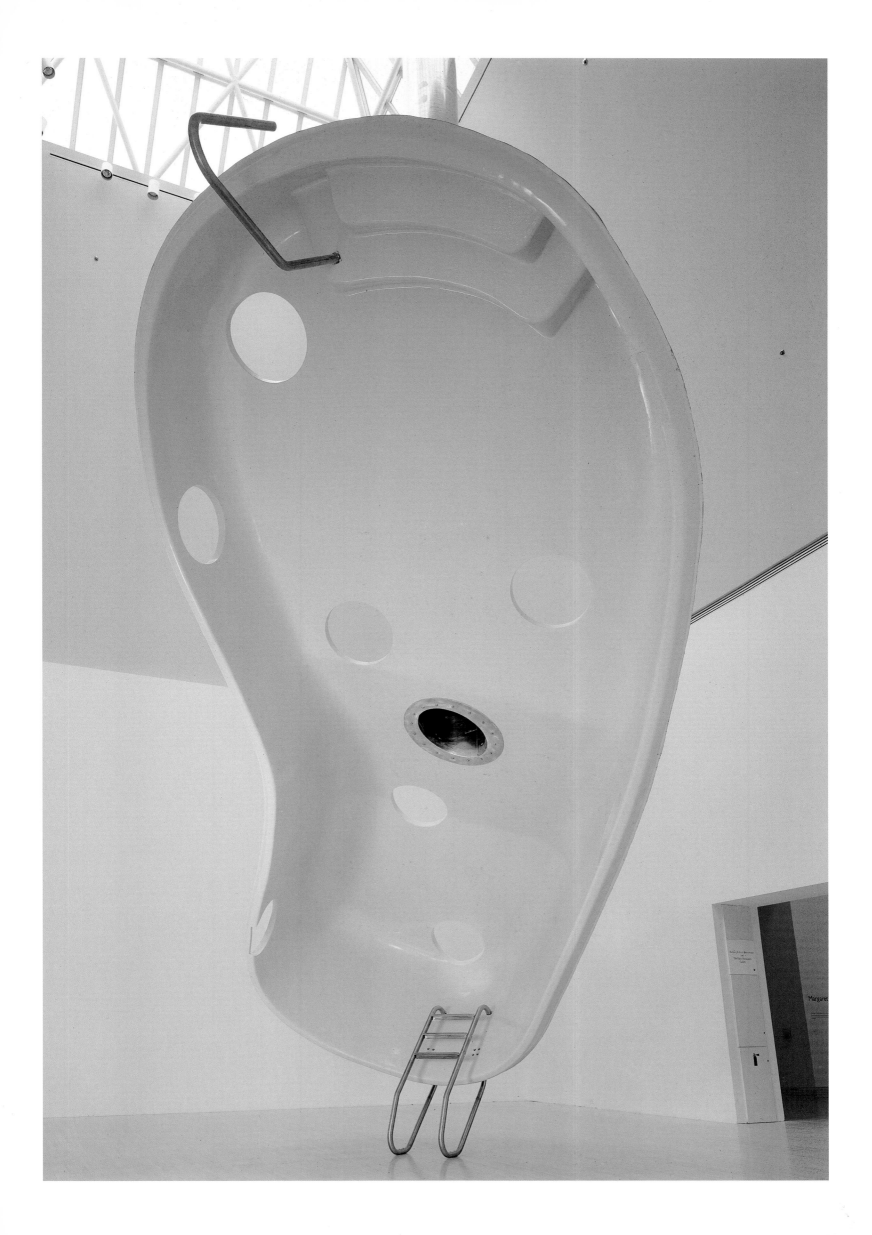

Cutting Corners 1995

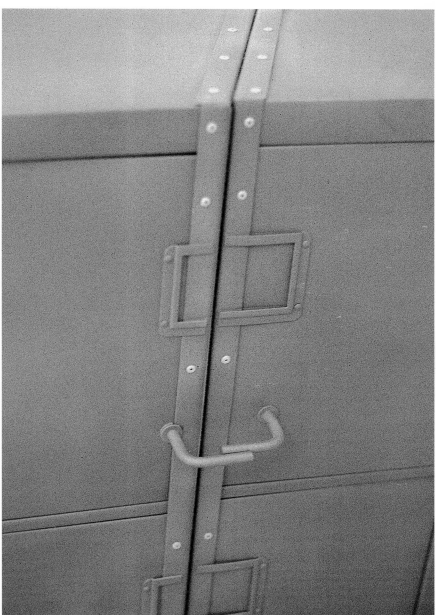

ROOM 6 CHANNEL VIEW HOTEL

42 **Doner** 1996

46   **Jamming Gears** 1996

Richard Wilson *Jamming Gears*
Serpentine Gallery, London
15 August – 15 September 1996

Photography by Martin Garcia Perez, Hugo Glendinning,
Robin Klassnik, Morton Thorkilsden, Stephen White,
Richard Wilson, Edward Woodman.
All photography until 1996 courtesy Matt's Gallery, London.

Curated by Jonathan Watkins, assisted by Suzanne Cotter

Catalogue designed and produced by Peter B. Willberg
Printed in England by The Pale Green Press

© Andrew Wilson and Richard Wilson

ISBN 18 70814 029